TRYING FOR PEACE:
SELF-ACTUALIZATION
WORLD
FEDERALISM

TRYING FOR PEACE:
SELF-ACTUALIZATION
AND WORLD
FEDERALISM

JOSEPH SASSOON

TRYING FOR PEACE:
SELF-ACTUALIZATION AND WORLD FEDERALISM

iUniverse books may be ordered through booksellers or by contacting:

iUniverse
1663 Liberty Drive
Bloomington, IN 47403
www.iuniverse.com
1-800-Authors (1-800-288-4677)

ISBN: 978-1-5320-3942-3 (sc)
ISBN: 978-1-5320-3941-6 (e)

Library of Congress Control Number: 2018900563

Print information available on the last page.

iUniverse rev. date: 10/24/2018

Contents

To the memory of my parents

Preface

This is the third book in a trilogy on self-actualization and world federalism. My interest in that subject dates back to my college years, when I got hooked on the idea of world federalism after attending a lecture by a renowned world federalist. Although I agreed with his aims, I did not think that there could be a world federalist government without a common value system. Union can occur only among nations with a common value system that guides their lives. This value system must come from nature, moreover, and not human volition. At that time, following WWII, there was an ideological struggle between the democratic countries on the one hand and communist countries on the other. This amounted to a struggle between classical democracy and arbitrary autocracy. I did not think that the two were reconcilable. In fact, I had no use for either, since there was no way to prove scientifically which one was right. Both were a question of inclination or human volition and not human nature.

This led me to search for knowledge of human nature, beginning with human motivation. The knowledge of human motivation, at that time, ended with Kurt Goldstein and Abraham Maslow. They postulated that human motivation is synonymous with the overall desire for self-actualization. Everyone needs to survive and grow, to strive for pleasure and avoid pain, to satisfy the hunger for food, sex, and other activities. All were part of the overall need for self-actualization. However, neither Goldstein nor Maslow showed how self-actualization could be achieved, let alone how to create a system of values that would guide people toward that goal. I made this task my own. I wanted to find out how self-actualization can be achieved and the value system that it requires. Only that kind of value system can guide all peoples toward world federalism.

My research into how self-actualizing works, unbeknownst to me at that time, became a lifetime research project that has involved decades of observing self-actualizers, both contemporary and historical. One of the most important results of my work was to bring about and unite all human sciences. So far, said sciences were mostly descriptive. The new hard sciences are predictive and encompass the whole range of human actions and thought. In this case, only those ideas that are grounded in the self-actualization for the greatest number of people within the context of the humanist code have any creditability, while all the others who lack this connection are confusing and unscientific. The first book of this trilogy, *Self-Actualization: Theory and Technology*, contained a new theory of motivation (see appendix A), and an entirely new discovery to explain how self-actualization is achieved. The second book, *The Humanist Society*, dealt with the social demands that are required to achieve self-actualization for the greatest number of people among any community or nation as it exists today. This work, the third book in my trilogy, shows how to spread self-actualization worldwide.

The humanist code (see appendix B) emerged as the axioms that are required to guide people toward self-actualization. Inevitably, there must be new political institutions, never before tried, to attain that goal. Indeed, the humanist code would be at the heart of any future struggles toward democratic and humanistic world federalism.

The main message of the humanist code is that only one

philosophy can unite all humans. That philosophy is derived from human nature and, therefore, is the only one that actually works. The task is not to evaluate one philosophy over another, therefore, but to distinguish between sharply defined definitions of good and evil.

Introduction

Self-actualization is the key to all social organizations. Why world federalism? Why now? The success of the American union, which has transformed the world in about two centuries in terms of the greatest personal freedom and history, the greatest prosperity ever known, has challenged the world in its attractiveness. Now every nation wants the same thing.

The same greatness has led to the production of weapons of mass destruction, which is rapidly spreading throughout the world, most ominously among predator dictators. An amount of plutonium the size of an apple in the hands of terrorists could kill or injure hundreds of thousands of innocent people. These are now waiting to be used, particularly against the leading democracies. Obviously, a new world order is needed to cope with this new situation. This would mean a drastic and unprecedented social change to our national and international order, all to the betterment and safety of the human conditions.

The secret of American success lies in its essentially humanistic values, which are congruent with individual self-actualization or human nature. And that, in turn, is universal. Those values must come from either religion or secular ideology. The United States has its largely Judeo-Christian system in its Protestant form. It also has a constitution and a political system, which, though not perfect, still work well in their consistency and flexibility.

Many countries have tried to imitate the United States in

their constitutions and political systems, notably South America, but they have not been successful. The reason for their failures lies in the lack of connection between the technology of self-actualization and the values required to produce it. In the case of the United States and other humanist democracies, they happen to connect. The purpose of this book is to show how to transfer values that lead to democracy as a function of self-actualization in the hands of a humanist democracy.

When society protects all people and encourages them to achieve their maximum potential and be rewarded for it, society gains freedom, wealth, and strength from the collective work of all its individuals. This, in turn, empowers them to achieve even greater things for society. And that, in turn, helps society achieve more than it would have, in a beneficent circle. This is how civilization rises and is nourished to maturity and further greatness.

On the other hand, if society thwarts personal self-actualization, it is diminished accordingly. This prevents people from achieving their maximum capacity, so society as a whole weakens and declines. It will one day fall victim to outside invasion or domination and disappear from history, such as the old Greek civilization.

The art and science of self-actualization have been amply described in book 1*of this trilogy. (For a summary of that theory, see appendix A.) Self-actualization is conceived by the humanist value. This is contained in the humanist code (see appendix B), which tells us how good and evil are formed relative to human nature or self-actualization. Equally important, it tells us how far we can pursue a good idea or a good system before modifying or abandoning it. Humanism is a worldview that leads to self-actualization for the greatest number of people in any society. It

---

* Joseph Sassoon, *Self-Actualization: Theory and Technology* (Montreal: Circle Books, 1988).

is derived from human nature, which makes it both innate and universal.

The present world political system is not working and is in danger of collapse, leading to species-threatening wars. What we need is a new system that is derived from human nature and suited to it, one that would then have the virtues of a humanist democracy, peace, and permanence.

As mentioned, this is the third book in a trilogy on self-actualization and world federalism. The trilogy contains a new theory of motivation in line with the work of Kurt Goldstein (1878–1965) and a new value system called the humanist code, which relies on the new theory of self-actualization by Goldstein. In this book, I discuss ways of bringing about a democratic world federalism that relies on the new theory of human motivation.

The social sciences at present are fractured and controversial because there is no acceptable theory of human nature that would unite all features of human nature. One theory defeats the previous one, and confusion reigns. The greater the fragmented knowledge of the human condition, the greater the confusion surrounding it due to lack of a unifying matrix. We know the nature of wheat and the nature of ants and horses but not that of humans. A theory comes and goes, but nothing definite has happened. All theories have hitherto been subject to human volition and not to a verifiable theory of human nature. The only exception has been the drive toward self-actualization postulated by Kurt Goldstein and Abraham Maslow (1908–1970). (See the first book of this trilogy.) In fact, the entelechial process (see glossary) of self-actualization is a natural given. Anything that happens (including human behavior) or does not happen affects the EP or the drive toward self-actualization. As the theory of human nature, it is verifiable as a united theory of human motivation (see appendix A). The EP is the source of all legitimate values.

Viewed from the prospective eyes of humanism, history at

its core is the struggle between good and evil. The good refers to all activities and events that support self-actualization within the context of the humanist code (see appendix B). Evil is what impedes self-actualization and includes all authoritarian and tyrannical regimes in particular.

Self-actualization entails three challenges. First, the personal, which means how people use their early life experiences in the interest of self-actualization (proper physical care, values, adequate education, the right social life, reproduction and family life, all of which I have described in the first book of this trilogy and summarized in appendix A).

The second challenge is our social system. Unless a social system is hospitable to and cooperative with personal self-actualization, frustration will set in. Society begins to weaken as self-actualization declines and wanes. A humanist society, as described in the second book of this trilogy, is essential to the self-actualization for the greatest number of people within that society.

The third challenge is international. In this case, it includes also the world as a whole, both human and nonhuman. That is the topic of this work. The international scene has a decisive effect not only on personal self-actualization but also on the future of civilization. Unity among humanist democracies is essential for maximizing the self-actualization for the greatest number of people. By *unity*, I mean extra strengths and opportunities in the face of any strident authoritarian challenge. The power of the union would be more than the sum total of its parts. Imagine the power of the American union of fifty states against fifty completely independent countries. It would not, of course, be the same. The great power of the United States in promoting democracy would not be there without a strong union. Similarly, union among the existing democracies would lead to an even stronger democratic block.

Common humanist values are what make any union possible.

Humanist values are derived from nature and are, therefore, universal. Applying them would prevent anyone from suffering or losing rights. On the contrary, everyone would gain in strength and thus contribute to the welfare of society. Under this system, all personal rights that existed before the union would be protected. These include language, religion, cultural expressions, and so on. The democratic union would settle all international disputes, too, through the application of the law, which would preclude authoritarianism and aggression.

The union would be in charge also of planetary health and protect future generations from a drastically degraded environment. The union would face many threats from authoritarian regimes, which, unlike democracies, are antihumanist. Authoritarian behavior does not derive from human nature, per se; it derives from human nature that has been perverted by dehumanizing cultural, political, or economic patterns. On the contrary, autocracy is derived from arbitrary forces, such as lies, and fosters brutal policies. Therefore, authoritarian regimes, when recognized, have no innate or intrinsic popular support. They produce oppressed or diluted populations waiting to be liberated. Authoritarian systems produce violence, such as war and terrorism, and usually take a heavy toll on democracies because of their arbitrary and sometimes pathogenic ideas. Their very raison d'être is to work against democracy either by trying to conquer it or in denying people democratic rights. These authoritarian systems have no right to exist because they impede human nature and growth. They present a real threat to humanism and must, therefore, be eliminated. Democracies become vulnerable to massive attacks by weapons of mass destruction. Without union, there is no future for democracy.

The union must have elected representatives from mature democracies, whose chief task would be to protect the human rights of its citizens in line with the humanist code and to spread those values to those who are deprived of them under authoritarian regimes.

The union of humanist democracies, as presented here, must not accept members unless their people are well educated in humanism. All people can learn the theory of humanism, but they require, in addition, the experience of democracy. Meanwhile, we can supply commercially organized administrations to supply government services to those who hope to establish democracies.

The strength of authoritarian systems does not lie in the number or loyalty of their citizens, because they have no free citizens. Their leaders could never match the power of united democracies and would eventually provoke revolutions from within. The existing followers of authoritarian dictators are victims of oppression but will eventually seek political freedom and economic prosperity under humanism.

The United Nations is a complete failure and cannot solve world problems because its members do not all adhere to the same value system. The democracies are a minority in the United Nations; authoritarian regimes are the majority. This explains the deadlock as well as the attacks against smaller democracies. The laws of this institution are not always enforceable and do not protect democracies against assaults from rogue nations.

In this book, I propose a new way of spreading democracy gradually, both in theory and practice, to those who still lack it. Once the union of democratic nations is established, it will become a strong magnet for people everywhere because this is how human nature works. It gravitates not only toward strength and prosperity but also away from tyranny and poverty.

The union of democratic states will offer to the new world a system of association by which any people of authoritarian states can choose to associate themselves with democratic states. It will be managed by newly created commercial expert organizations specializing in government administration within the context of the humanist code. Governments will no longer be under the thumb of dictators. This will be an entirely new system dawning on a new world.

Human behavior, as I explained in the first book, is two-dimensional. It consists of a purpose—sometimes subconscious—and the means to achieve that purpose. This is expressed as follows:

Behavior (A) the purpose / Means (B)

I find it helpful to express some forms of action in terms of ends and means (see glossary), thus discouraging anyone from confusing the two. This leads to greater precision in describing specific behaviors.

I should like to explain some terms that I introduced in the last two books, namely the Greek term *entelechy* (see glossary). This refers to innate behavior coming from nature of all living things. The entelechial process (EP) is derived from the entelechy and refers to the process by which the entelechy works. On the matter of how the entelechial process actually works, please see appendix A of this work.

The axioma complex (constant A1) (see glossary) is a form of knowledge consisting of the religio-ideological system that determines national values. It is a system of knowledge that requires no verification but provides first principles as in the logical-deductive system. It plays a large role in behavior. Second is a personal values system (constant A2), which refers to the values of the individual. This is different from constant A1 but partakes of the same type of knowledge; like the axioma complex, it requires no verification. Only the (humanist or antihumanist) implications matter.

An important element in this book is the humanist code, which is described in appendix B. It is derived from the great religions in so far as they refer to self-actualization for the greatest number of people. It was designed to distinguish good from evil values objectively and scientifically, which we now need. It is also designed to tell us how far we can pursue a good idea before abandoning it. This subject has been amply covered in the first two books of this trilogy.

Axiopathy (see glossary) is the use of religion or political ideology for criminal or tyrannical purposes. It opposes human values that serve good purposes.

This is the time par excellence for democratic world federalism. The world might not seem ready for this political novelty, but this self-actualization for the greatest number of people within the context of the humanist code remains the greatest good. The greatest good must determine what is politically and socially correct or advantageous under any circumstances. The proposed institutions that I discuss in this book are what we need to produce the greatest good for our time. This project will require adjustment to new values and new political institutions. The proposed changes function as part of an outline of what we must do, not a blueprint for achieving them. To attempt a more ambitious plan at this time would endanger the entire project.

CHAPTER 1

Why World Federalism? Why Now?

The world is moving toward unification, but it is characterized by two opposing value systems. One is the humanist value system (see appendix B). Opposing that is the authoritarian value system (see chapter 6), which denies the right to self-actualization and postulates the prior rights of rulers to determine all policies. These two systems are incompatible and thus in continual conflict. This is demonstrated in the history of the United Nations, where a democratic minority faces an overwhelming majority of nondemocratic or pseudo-democratic states. Only a union of humanist democracies could counteract that majority. The United Nations should be disbanded like the old League of Nations was. It is incapable of solving complex world problems and thus poses a danger to world security and stability.

Unity among people with values in common is not only beneficial to all but necessary for any society. It leads to greater power than the sum total of the democratic union as a whole. It not only increases this power as a whole but also creates a new reality that is completely beyond the earlier one as separate entities. This is exemplified, as we said before, by the union of American states to form the United States of America, which have embedded in their separate constitutions similar humanistic values.

One of the greatest tasks of a new union would be protecting the environment. The existing union tolerates despoliation of the environment by exploiting fossil fuels and polluting the air and the rain forests. Only a world government, a higher authority than any national government, could plan and implement policies to deal with this global problem by balancing human rights and economics with planetary health.

Perhaps the most important motive for a new union of democratic countries is warding off the common threat to democracy from militarily aggressive authoritarian countries. The latter forced democracies into the numerous wars that have led to heavy losses of both life and material wealth. The loss of material wealth leads inevitably to the steady hemorrhaging of democratic power and therefore to the triumph of tyranny with all its dangers. The new union of democracies would create enough power to topple the dictators. It would eliminate war by its very power to squash any aggression toward democratic member countries.

A new democratic union would not only lead to the expansion of democracy throughout the world but also commit itself to the eradication of authoritarianism and, therefore, to the liberation of all humankind. But would all people benefit from a system of human rights derived from nature, or would some continue to ensure the system that opposes those rights? The problem becomes too immense to settle peacefully without the managing hand of a single democratic world government acting in the interest of all humanity and not merely those of the strongest members.

All humans are naturally motivated by the desire for self-actualization, so we must ensure that all-embracing instinct becomes the engine of history. When self-actualization is opposed by law, people tend to react destructively. Some seek political power for themselves or new places to conquer. But when self-actualization is fostered by law, people achieve their goals peacefully. They embrace their potential and, if necessary, are ready to risk their lives in its defense. Potentially all people are humanistic by nature. This is an important trend in history. It must ultimately prevail if humans are to endure as a species on this planet. This will not be easy to ensure, because it requires major shifts in the formation of public institutions. But this new system is bolstered by the central fact of self-actualization. This goal is the constant that must determine the existence and evolution of all institutions. They are valuable to the extent that they achieve one empirical goal—but in ways that we can correct in case of error.

CHAPTER 2

Democracy as Function of Self-Actualization

Democracy is not merely a political system; it is a function of self-actualization. It is a special knowledge that relies on the drive toward self-fulfillment. Under humanism, it is a special technology that anyone can and must learn. Among the first and foremost important parts of this technology is the axioma complex, or value system. For democracy to survive, people must see or feel its direct connection with self-actualization. This is a process through which democratically inclined people come together due to a common biological interest. And various social media outlets offer the best collective medium for this process to spread. Social media would be very effective in spreading humanist or democratic principles.

Social media is now unregulated, and this leads to misrepresentation and authoritarian propaganda, including terrorist propaganda. The humanist convention here would be able to sort out the good from the bad. In any case, the humanist message cannot afford to stay away from such a powerful method of spreading its vital message. In the end, humanism will win by exposing the flaws, if necessary, with powerful messages of truth.

The humanist code (see appendix B) postulates that the function of government is to foster the self-actualization within every community. It bans authoritarianism to the extent that any authoritarian system prevents the self-actualization for the greatest number of people.

Democracy is not merely majority rule, although this is a necessary part of the whole system (as are separated judicial, legislative, and executive branches of government). The primary function of democracy is to foster self-actualization. It relies on a special political system.

At the core of democratic knowledge is the humanist code. Without the strong motivation for self-actualization, there can be no genuine democracy. There would be no need for it. The lack of democratic knowledge creates a vacuum, allowing any authoritarian system, either old or new, to infect democratic institutions.

Modern democracies went through many decades of trial and error before achieving a passable democratic system. These democracies acquired humanist value through religion, primarily the Judeo-Christian tradition at present, in its Protestant form. Those values inspire people to maintain freedom at all costs and have led to a high degree of self-actualization. Not surprisingly, they have led also to the popularity of democracy and vigorous opposition to authoritarianism. These are the characteristics of healthy living and natural fulfillment.

The best way to spread democracy is to learn about self-actualization in a context of healthy living and freedom. This knowledge of human motivation is contained in the unified theory of motivation (see appendix A). This is not difficult to do, by linking self-actualization with humanist values. The latter influences and guides people to the former. That is the basis of democracy. In this book, I have described those values in secular terms to make them accessible to everyone. The humanist code is universal, but it is congruent with all major religions and derived from them to the extent that they are correctly interpreted in line with the full-fledged technology of self-actualization, which contains the precise method for achieving that goal.

Other self-actualization technologies follow easily from the technologies that I discuss here. During my discussion of these technologies, the role of values becomes evident as a guide toward the great and liberating goal of self-actualization.

It is not enough for a few elite citizens to understand and accept democracy. They would soon be corrupted and attracted to authoritarianism if ordinary people or voters were to fail in following the same values. So the humanist value system goes hand in hand with human nature and thus includes both the elite and the masses. This must be part of the educational system in every country that wants to become, or remain, democratic. It must be spread through the mass media. The evil of despotism must clearly be contrasted with the benefits of humanist democracy so that the choice becomes as clear and self-evident as the one between physical health and disease. Where humanist values are not yet established in any given country seeking democracy, it may take up to two or three generations before humanist values become culturally embedded in that society. Eventually, humanist values will triumph over authoritarian ones, no matter how deeply entrenched the latter might be, because humanist values such as justice, freedom, and compassion are congruent with the better and normal part of human nature; authoritarian values such as tyranny, injustice, and deception, on the other hand, are opposed. Humanist values lead to well-being and triumph over suffering and evil. No people who understand this would revert to the distortion and perversion of the authoritarian system.

Nevertheless, a union of democratic and humanist countries would allow only new members that have had at least one generation of stable humanist democracy. Until then, these new members would be under the control of more experienced countries (which I discuss in chapter 5). This is to protect the democratic union.

7

These new democracies must not dilute the humanist character of the older ones. Only mature democracies would be called de jure members. Others would be de facto members. This is to indicate that de jure governments have established their legitimacy and are, therefore, competent to govern and control their national and international affairs. Only they would qualify for full membership in the union.

As I have already said, mature democracies have acquired their essential values from religions. To the extent that these religions have been correct, they have worked to produce stronger democracies.

CHAPTER 3
Who Qualifies?

The purpose of world federalism is self-actualization for the greatest number of people within the context of the humanist code. It must be reduced to a hard science. This requires two steps: first, the theoretical abstract part, which is represented in this case by the humanist code (see appendix B). The second step is the degree of self-actualization resulting from the application of the abstract section, which would be the objective, empirical, or real part. The latter is the only reality that we can depend on and the only verification of the abstract section. If a principle derived from the humanist code does not lead to the maximum degree of self-actualization, in any circumstances, it should be abandoned in favor of a better result within the same humanist code. Therefore, an abstract principle means nothing without the actual empirical result in terms of self-actualization. It is easy to write a long list of abstract rights without a corresponding result in terms of self-actualization in the real world. The real world shows the extent to which those rights are affected. Many people think that producing a great-sounding system of human rights in the abstract form ensures each exact application. This is false, as the Soviet constitution has clearly shown. It contains the words *democracy* and *basic rights*, which were not only unenforced but openly violated. Hence, the abstract section alone is worthless without a corresponding confirmation to the degree of self-actualization resulting from it. At present, most democracies are primarily on the abstract level.

The existing democracies, including the United States, are abstract and subject to various interpretations. The reason they sometimes work so well in fostering self-actualization is that they absorbed the underlying humanist values that originated in the Judeo-Christian tradition. Underlying these democracies are not only the abstract principles of constitutions but also the objective desire for self-actualization that emerged even earlier as interpretations of religious texts. These interpretations would have to be changed if any authoritarian regime were to replace democracy. And that could happen because all interpretations are possible at the abstract level: pro and con from the same religion or political system. The empirical method, on the other hand, is solidly and directly based on self-actualization. This empirical method cannot be altered effectively without objective evidence. The existing democracies rely, unfortunately, on abstract principles that sometimes rely, in turn, more on willful interpretations than on empirical evidence. It is not too difficult for interpreters to shift ever so slowly into the authoritarian mode, if so desired, while claiming to be humanists. This could lead to a fully authoritarian system. Only the solid evidence of self-actualization could prevent such a slow shift toward an authoritarian system (which is what happened to the once great Islamic civilization during the Middle Ages) and protect the nation from disastrous loss of rights. This means that every law must exhibit either a positive or a negative relation to self-actualization within the context of the humanist code.

Self-actualization is above the law. The primary function of the law is to supply the means for achieving it. Anything other than that may lead to tyranny. Idealization of the law against the emotional attachment to self-actualization often leads to severe injustice. The law, if it remains just, must support the stronger and more important emotional issues of self-fulfillment. Self-actualization is the master, and the law its servant.

Thus, an abstract proposition in the American Constitution states that "all members are created equal." But that was interpreted to exclude a recognizable minority in the Dred Scott case. Empirical evidence, as the criteria, would never have supported the exclusion of black people from the status of equality.

Logically, we can assume that a principle derived from a given proposition is true because it must be contained in that proposition. But this is not always so. The premise could be infiltrated by contrary ideas due to reinterpretation, which is what happened to Dred Scott. The result of that case was to bypass, for black people, the principles of equality, life, liberty, and the pursuit of happiness as enshrined in the Constitution.

A good abstract system like the American Constitution can last for a few centuries at most, but it will eventually wear out in the process of reinterpretation. Congress reinterpreted the Constitution to forbid the production, consumption, and ownership of alcohol, for example, which is what led to Prohibition. The new empirical technology guarantees the preservation of human rights. Given the empirical method of humanism, only policies that foster self-actualization are legitimate and, therefore, proper measurements of all other proposed policies. Self-actualization is not an abstract notion but an empirically verifiable one. And this becomes a matter of basic rights for all. The abstract system on which current democracy relies must be shifted to the empirical and concrete one of humanism. Any misinterpretation would be the interpreter's own responsibility. Those who violate empirical principles would do so at their own risk. This is the only way to ensure the health and permanence of a good society. In this way, human rights rely not only on legislation but also on science.

At present, most advanced democratic countries qualify

for membership in the proposed humanist democratic world federation. Newer applicants must require at least twenty-five years of democratic experience and a standard of living that does not threaten the standards of existing democratic countries. Every country should control its immigration policy, too, with this in mind.

A new union of democratic countries would be responsible for the care of the environment. This would be one of its chief tasks. The union would likewise be responsible for establishing a military force, preferably of volunteers, to enforce its peaceful policy. This would replace all other military forces. This new force would be vastly different from anything that the United Nations has produced so far. It would resemble the American Armed Forces.

Meanwhile, a common value system would ensure its influence in the international sphere. There would be no loss of existing rights by uniting with other democracies; on the contrary, uniting with them would substantially increase rights. The whole would be greater, in other words, than the sum total of its parts. The same would be true of this new union's military might, cultural diversity, and economic advance. There would be no loss of national identity, yet a new and stronger international identity would emerge. This would not be like the European Union, which is not based on humanist values, because these alone would form the strongest unity. Most of the existing European states are not ready for humanist democracy and would, therefore, not initially qualify as full members of the new humanist union being proposed here. In short, the existing European Union lacks the cement of the humanist values and close economic status. The new union would be based on its own humanist values and nearly equal economic conditions.

The voting would be done by elected citizens of the union. There would be a new tier of elected representatives and administrators as well as a judicial branch of the government. The latter would be independent of the legislative and executive branches.

A union congruent with the humanist code would endure because it would be based on human nature. It would increase the power of the whole.

CHAPTER 4

Client-Country System

Although the peoples of most countries would like to join a democratic union and live under a system of humanist values, they are not necessarily ready to assume the responsibility of membership. Those people could join as client-countries: territories to be governed and protected by the union as a whole. The important thing is that the political relationship is consensual and could be ended after a period of approximately five years after a vote in the client-country. In other words, this relationship is not like a colonial one. It is a free political association that depends on mutual interest. These client-countries would enjoy political and economic benefits while remaining free from the threat of internal autocracy or foreign invasion.

Economic benefits coupled with personal freedom would inevitably lead to the elimination of poverty and the rise of healthy and growing middle classes. These countries would have the advantages of a humanist system without losing their independence. When they reach a predetermined standard of political and economic development, they could apply to join the union as full members. If not accepted for any reason, they could withdraw their applications for membership and return to the status of unaffiliated countries.

Meanwhile, the union would benefit from expanding its

democracy and increasing its territories, natural resources, and population. In colonial systems, there was no schedule for independence. In this case, client-countries could leave at any time they choose to do so, after either popular votes or after their contractual periods. Secondly, the client-countries would be protected by rights within the context of the humanist code. Apart from those contractual rights in favor of the client-countries, the latter would be free to leave.

Administering client-countries would be a special cadre of men and women with specialized training (which I discuss in chapter 5). They would be from any country and earn money for their services, paid at the same rates as any other professionals or experts in their own fields. There would be no special privileges by virtue of their professional status. They would at all times be bound by the humanist code.

The art of government would be taught in professional schools. Graduates would be appointed by the union to serve in various capacities and be paid on the basis of results. They would be collectively responsible for the whole administration and for the achievements of its programs.

The immediate aim would not necessarily be to raise the standard of living to that of member-countries but to make the most of human and natural resources available locally and, therefore, not only to eliminate poverty but also to ensure security and human rights. Meanwhile, the union would not be forced to lower its standard of living while helping client-countries. The latter, moreover, would protect their own immigration policies.

In due course, these countries would learn the theory and practice of humanist democracy as described in the previous chapter. This would promote their human dignity and qualify them for union with other democracies.

One important result of the client-country system would be the prevention of large population shifts from poor countries to rich ones (a major problem in the early twenty-first century). This is because the standard of living would rise in client-countries. Mass migration from the poverty and oppression of sending countries places a great challenge to the economies of receiving countries. The union would be able to solve these problems.

New countries would be attracted by the prospect of enforced human rights and would thus avoid traumatic events such as the Arab Spring uprising of 2010. A humanist union would not conflict with distinctive forms of nationalism because it would release the energies of the people toward creative (humanist) endeavors. Imagine—the whole Syrian civil war of the early twenty-first century could have been avoided had there been a democratic government under the control of the people instead of a vicious dictator.

CHAPTER 5
The Commercial Administration

When only the members of a small elite understand how democracy works, they cannot achieve it. Informed citizens must support and correct, if necessary. For client-countries, however, it would be possible for the elite to hire for-profit administrations under the trusteeship of the humanist democratic union. There is the need for professional administrators to manage governments. They would function like business corporations. Their task would be to govern in ways that foster self-actualization for the greatest number of people within the context of the humanist code. This would be similar to foreign experts, such as medical or agricultural administrators, working under local governments. These civilian experts would give client-countries the humanist planning and direction that they need to make progress on human rights.

The system would have a fixed period of four to five years under the terms of a contractual obligation to achieve specific goals and, in return, be paid by the treasury but supplemented if necessary by loans from the union. In the meantime, client-countries would have the benefits of humanist and democratic governments.

The system would be controlled by the union government and would provide the same security and benefits that it would to full members. In this way, client-countries would be protected against incipient dictatorships even before qualifying as humanist democracies.

New democracies that seek full membership in the union would have opportunities either to change commercial officials periodically or to extend their service for additional terms. This would give client-countries the same opportunities for good government as full members. These benefits would make dictatorship more unattractive than it already is—except, perhaps, for dictatorships that rely on nationalism or some other technology that thrills the masses. Furthermore, it would give those states who are free to join allies in the struggle to prevent invaders.

This is indeed a new way to advance the cause of good government in countries that are not quite ready for it. They could learn by observing foreign experts (just as they do now in connection with other technologies, such as agriculture or medicine). The humanist code would protect citizens from exploitation. In due course, when they are ready to maintain democratic institutions, they will be able to join the union as full members if they so desire. Gradually, humanist democracies would spread. Eventually they would become universal. Authoritarianism would thus be wiped out. From then on, international disputes would be settled by law, not violence or war.

This type of government, though untried, is both possible and desirable in our time to save countries from maladministration or being overrun internally and exploited.

CHAPTER 6

The Authoritarian System: A Common Threat

The primary purpose of a union of democracies would be to liberate countries from despotism and thus free them for the benefits of self-actualization. All people want to attain self-actualization, and democracies can help them do so. The main cause of enslavement is lack of access to a special type of knowledge that only humanist democracies can foster. People must learn that the source of self-actualization is within human nature. Religions have understood this, although they have not used secular language to describe human nature. Here is one example. The American founders produced a society that valued the work ethic, which originated in the Calvinist version of Protestantism. The same ethic, translated into secular terms, is part of the humanist code (as you can see in appendix B).

All human rights originate in the universal drive for self-actualization. I describe the technology of self-actualization in the first book of this trilogy. Moreover, it is contained in the unified theory of motivation (which I present in appendix A). The first step toward democracy, therefore, is learning how self-fulfillment actually works by recognizing the vital role of not only humanist democracy but also the international order that fosters precisely the same goal—that is, self-actualization. Once people learn this, human rights emerge automatically.

It is easy to understand and assimilate the technology of self-actualization because it represents a part of everyday human behavior and consciousness. If self-actualization is the purpose of life, which means that no one can live without it, then it follows that the right of self-actualization is absolute and basic to human survival. It becomes a natural and essential part of living and, therefore, beyond denial. Only when the great majority of people accept this premise does democracy become possible. Otherwise, democracy remains meaningless, vague, or unattainable. Humanist democracy acquires its power from its understanding of human nature, which explains its mission to spread the word among those living under dictatorships.

Fortunately, modern technologies, notably social media, make it possible to spread this knowledge widely and quickly, in addition to other methods of communication. And it is in the interest of existing democracies to spread that knowledge to other countries in order to acquire the additional power of liberated peoples. No authoritarian system would be able to withstand the competing attraction of democracy.

The difference between the humanist democracy and authoritarianism, as I say, is that the former derives its legitimacy from human nature and the second imposes arbitrary systems that suit the interests of rulers, which means that it uses violence to oppose self-actualization.

As far as humanists are concerned, the authoritarian system violates the EP and, therefore, has no right to exist. Actually, giving dictators the same rights as other citizens would amount to a denial of those same rights to those other citizens. That would be like recognizing the right of a tumor to grow within the body like any other organ. In both cases, it is an invitation to destroy the healthier part. Indeed, humanist democracy would ultimately require the eradication of dictatorships worldwide.

At present, in 2018, authoritarian systems have democratic ones by the throat. They do not follow the rules of war as recognized by the democracy and thus have tactical advantages. Worse, many democracies tend to appease dictatorships with concessions in order to avoid war. But appeasement does not work. On the contrary, it encourages and stimulates the aggressive impulses of dictators. Nothing makes dictatorships more dangerous and violent than appeasement.

Predatory sociopaths are the most extreme and dangerous despots. They recognize no obligation to limit their power and cruelty. And their power lies in violating every rule of behavior that traditional and democratic societies recognize. They can do anything, no matter how much suffering they cause. Examples from the twentieth century and the early twenty-first include Adolf Hitler, Joseph Stalin, Pol Pot, Saddam Hussein, Bashar al-Assad, and Kim Jong-un.

These people know nothing of normal human values or emotions. Their behavior is entirely motivated by constant D2 (which I discussed in connection with the unified theory of motivation—see appendix A). Being antihumanist, they cannot claim normal humanist rights. We must not risk millions of lives in order to save or serve the interest of one dictator.

The struggle against the authoritarian tyranny is a very ancient one, dating back to the Neolithic period. Only the rise of world religions and their ethical systems has curbed it. Measured against human history, the struggle against authoritarianism has just begun.

Some highly religious people and strong believers in God have abandoned their faith because they could not understand how God would allow such atrocities as the Holocaust. I do not pretend to know the mind of God on everything, but I do know that authoritarian systems are the true causes of these atrocities. Therefore, atrocities are human problems. We can solve them just as we can cure smallpox, polio, tuberculosis, and other plagues. We now know that if we do not want to repeat twentieth-century and twenty-first-century genocide, we must destroy authoritarian regimes root and branch. Otherwise, they will destroy us.

Knowledge is power—for both the greatest good and the greatest evil. As human knowledge and power increases, our power for good becomes limitless. And so does our power for evil. The capacity to destroy many or even all humans is a matter of technology. When these weapons of mass destruction become available, dictators can use them. Therefore, there is no alternative to instituting a democratic and humanist world government to manage our affairs safely, humanely, rationally, and lawfully.

One of the reasons for evil, such as the Holocaust, is free will. Without free will, humans could not serve the will of God through self-actualization. The choice between the God axiom on the level of the axioma complex (constant A1–A2) and the no-God axiom is empirical—how they affect self-actualization. This is an empirical problem, and the solution lies in examining the beliefs of self-actualizers to see which side wins this contest. We must remember that we are dealing with axioms or first principles to guide our lives and not isolated facts. All the evidence available now shows that the God axiom is far superior to the no-God axiom in ordering our human lives.

CHAPTER 7
The Two Faces of Colonialism

Colonialism has been demonized as evil, while history shows that some of the greatest events for good have been accomplished under colonialism. In fact, I mean the limited spread of self-actualization, including advancement in human rights and the control of malignant authoritarian powers. So some forms of colonialism, though by no means all (or at all times), have left behind some good legacies (such as traditions of parliamentary democracy, just legal systems, and so on). Authoritarian rule, however, is inherently evil. It ravages countries where self-actualization is either weak or barely present. Those who demonize colonialism have helped authoritarian systems, particularly those of communism and internal terrorism, by posing as liberators. In fact, I suggest, that they are exploiters and oppressors themselves, far worse than the actual colonizers. They successfully hide behind antique colonist slogans. They are par excellence the new colonizers, exploiters, and tyrants, not the liberators that they pretend to be. It is thus about time to review the good and bad features of colonialism through humanist eyes as described above.

Some forms of colonialism, such as that of the British, planted the seed of democracy; others, such as that of the Spanish, promoted authoritarianism.

The colonialism of Great Britain led indirectly to the creation of the United States of America, which is now the greatest democracy in history, and other humanist democracies such as Canada, Australia, New Zealand, and Israel. The most important legacy of "good colonialism" is the transmission of humanist values, however, which is the essential basis of democracy. This transmission took place under the aegis of the Judeo-Christian value system, which directly or indirectly encouraged colonized people to emulate specific Western traditions. In addition, good colonialism transmitted educational, government, industrial, and commercial methods. Good colonialism acted as an instrument of democracy and led to greater freedom despite its flaws and setbacks. Change is now underway. Even good colonialism has some serious flaws, after all. But these did not cancel out the benefits of democracy, prosperity, and human rights over the long term. Without good colonialism, there would have been few democracies.

Bad colonial regimes were brutal and exploitive, although even these have left behind some basics that can lead to democracy. Among the victims of bad colonialism are the Latin American countries as well as China, Burma, and some others, many of which have succumbed to authoritarian power since independence.

On the whole, good or bad colonial regimes have acted as mediators in the historic events leading to a global civilization. In some cases, colonialism ended too quickly, leaving a vacuum that was filled by dictators, such as in Zimbabwe, Libya, and much of the Middle East. On the whole, newly "liberated" countries are still corrupt and tyrannical. They would all benefit from the establishment of a strong humanist democratic world union.

Humanist values are a prerequisite of democracy and must add up to the equivalent of a religious quest. Those values are now flowing over the globe due to colonialism, despite some of the ugly results of colonialism. The good side effects of colonialism have played a vital, albeit controversial role in human advancement. And this current continues to grow, sometimes underground, toward its end of liberating the populations.

CHAPTER 8

Self-Actualization as the Matrix of Human Behavior and Institutions

Self-actualization is the matrix of all human activities. Nothing one does or does not do ever escapes that matrix. This single fact greatly simplifies our understanding of human behavior. Beyond this matrix is only the confusion of conflicting or disorderly ideas.

The first technology is the personal: providing everyone with the means of achieving self-actualization. I discussed this topic in the first book of this trilogy. It is abbreviated in appendix A of this work.

The second technology is collective: engineering and creating society in ways that lead to the self-actualization for the greatest number of people. I discussed that technology in the second book.

Both could be implemented immediately without causing social upheaval.

This third technology is international. This might appear difficult, but it is much simplified in connection with the notion of self-actualization. Everything, including every national and international organization, must promote self-actualization and evolve in relation to it. The central requirement for self-actualization is to know how far we can follow good ideas, such as patriotism, sovereignty, capitalism, socialism, feminism, democracy, and so on, and when to accommodate the more important entelechial process. (See appendix B.)

Let us start with patriotism. The humanist face of patriotism is vastly different from the authoritarian one. According to the first humanist manifestation, it is constructed and peaceful, all inclusive, nonhostile, and democratic. This form of patriotism is essential for self-actualization on the social scale.

On the other hand, authoritarian patriotism is hostile, repressive, and tyrannical, denying self-actualization in favor of glorifying the personality of the ruler or rulers. It is the main support of the authoritarian system. It does not value human life or any human rights beyond what the ruler allows. It is, therefore, highly destructive. An example of humanist patriotism is that of Jews. For two thousand years of exile, the Jewish people kept contributing significantly to civilization while keeping alive the hope of return from exile. Authoritarian patriotism, on the other hand, places no value on the lives or self-actualization of the people but only on the power and interest of the leaders.

The same applies to capitalism, which is essential to a good and healthy society. On the other hand, if too much capital accumulates in the hands of the few, democracy becomes asphyxiated, and despotism or plutocracy begins to perceptively take hold. This causes democracy to die. Deciding how far we can allow capital to accumulate in the hands of the few must depend, according to humanism, on empirical conditions that vary in time and place. Therefore, humanism encourages and supports healthy capitalism but forbids plutocracy or the rule of money, which is authoritarian and destructive.

In this way, the humanist code tells us how far we can go with good ideas before they become toxic and must hence be modified or abandoned. This applies not only to nationalism or capitalism, as an example, but to all rewarding activities in life.

We must distinguish scientifically between good and evil in a way that transcends human volition. Once we understand human nature and follow its course, it becomes possible to achieve that important goal. In brief, all values or activities that lead to self-actualization for the greatest number of people within the context of the humanist code are inherently good; all values or activities that oppose self-actualization are evil.

Values and activities change in time and place. What is virtuous one day can become destructive another; therefore, we must not blindly follow any values all the time and in all places. For example, we know that telling lies in general is not good, but telling a lie in the service of a just cause is necessary and the lesser of two evils. Telling the truth that defeats self-actualization is not virtuous. Therefore, it is always the implication of value either for or against self-actualization that determines what is good or evil in any given situation or practice. We must not speak of any given value as being absolutely good or evil except in terms of what it does to self-actualization for the greatest number of people within the context of the humanist code.

Also involved in this category is the physical health of our planet. Only a humanist world government representing the opinions of both voting and nonvoting members would make decisions respecting the lives of humankind. This is a major problem in international affairs.

It is obvious that the foremost task of the new international order would be to ensure the unity of mature democracies, which share a common value derived from human nature and face common threats from authoritarian and lawless systems. The second task is to set up a client-country system, which would make it possible for any country to adopt and maintain a humanist and democratic system. Democracy presupposes a value system derived from human nature and is therefore universal. Under this system, the union of democratic countries could not be challenged by any authoritarian power. In fact, those suffering under despotism would be introduced to the same standards of freedom and prosperity as those already enjoying them.

The existing international order is dangerously chaotic. It favors the power of the authoritarian systems. It encourages conflict and terrorism. Democratic countries operate under one value system, while authoritarian ones operate under a completely different one. Democratic countries appear weak and indecisive in the eyes of despots. By contrast, the authoritarian system is aggressive and threatening. Democratic countries try to avoid war by what they call "diplomatic means," which sometimes amounts to appeasing the more dynamic dictators. This makes the latter more ambitious, dangerous, and aggressive than ever. Ultimately, this confusion can lead to war. With weapons of mass destruction being perfected every day, the results would be catastrophic not only to civilization but also to the human species and all life on the planet.

Self-actualization is the only permanent solution to conflict. No other solution will work. Humanists relate all conflicts to the matrix of self-actualization and find orderly and easily applicable solutions to all existing problems big or small. All complexities are revealed as simple because they are derived from human nature. If one humanist solution appears unworkable, another can be tried until the best nonauthoritarian solution possible is achieved.

CHAPTER 9
O for One World

O is for one world, the symbol of humanist world federalism. *O* is also a circle, which is the symbol of humanism. It likewise denotes its origin in human nature or self-actualization. The drive for self-actualization does not depend on human volition. It is a natural given and, therefore, common to all humans. All values leading to self-actualization and all rules for behavior are derived from that single constant. All behavior is empirically verifiable in terms of the degree to which it serves self-actualization. "*O* for one world," therefore, simply means that we are all one in our strive for self-actualization, and we all seek to achieve that most precious goal in life. No matter what divides us, we are united by that universal instinct. Therefore, all our rights are derived from that one thing. We are all equal by virtue of necessity. Therefore, all rights derived from the entelechial process (EP) are natural givens. They indicate the difference between what is right or wrong. That EP is the source of all values. Without it, we could not discern the difference between good and evil. Good values simply describe those that lead to self-actualization; bad values are ones that lead in the opposite direction and are therefore evil. Truth, for example, is a factor of self-actualization within the context of the humanist code. Good values are what we should do to achieve our goals. In this way, we experience values as good or evil.

The letter *O*, which can be formed with the index and thumb fingers is a symbol of humanism and can function as a salutation and recognition of humanism and world federalism. This symbol expresses fundamental respect for the best that human nature can be, and the salutation is a proclamation and affirmation of that fact. It is also marked on the Morse code as – – –.

Self-actualization is the realization of all good capacities in each of us. The primary capacity is spiritual, that which gives direction, aspirations, values, and overall planning for life. This is the function of constant A1, which unites people in a common endeavor. This is what makes them "one," and it trumps all other constants in the long term. Hence, this is the function of constant A1 or religion. There are those who believe that religion is a passing thing that will eventually disappear. But religion is an existing and necessary biological instinct and, therefore, cannot disappear. It might for a short time be replaced by a secular worldview but not for long. Because without a humanist religion, behavior becomes distorted. Ignoring religion would amount to ignoring any other genuine instinct such as the desire for food or sex, but it takes longer to manifest its absence.

Minor constant A2 is the conscience, which represents personal values as distinct from the group values of minor constant A1. These personal values may differ from group values.

All of these behaviors are derived from the EP within the context of the humanist code. The human organism is two-sided. When it is good, it is exceedingly good. This is the natural state for humans. But when it is bad, it is highly destructive and possibly suicidal, whether personally or collectively. Normally, the drive toward self-actualization has the upper hand. It is the source of life. It guides people to do what is right and good and repels them instinctively from doing what is wrong or evil. In that sense, it contains a healthy humanist spirit within the gift of free will. This is how human beings should function. History should encourage humans to function that way and has, on the whole, been moving in the right direction. There is no argument about the direction of the movement. The good moves two steps forward and one backward. Therefore, on the whole, we move forward. This gives us hope that a union of mature democracies can take place within one or two generations as a start toward eventual humanist world federalism.

At present, mature democracies rely primarily on abstract principles such as freedom, justice, democracy, and so on. But these are subject to interpretation, which could be anti-humanist, as they have been so many times in the past. Systems of government can rely on the empirically verifiable ideas of self-actualization, which are certain guides to what is the greatest good and, therefore, what will endure. Therefore, ideological and political systems must follow the empirical method and not be stranded in the murky area of abstraction alone. Only through self-actualization can humanities become a hard science. Abstraction works for democracy now because of incidental humanist values that democratic cultures contain. It might not always be so. Therefore, political systems must follow not abstract principles but hard science—that is, what works best for self-actualization for the greatest number of people. What works best would be a system that relies on concrete self-actualization. This would require a new order and thus become a part of collective self-actualization. All earlier systems (such as nationalism, colonialism, socialism, feminism, and so on) must now be absorbed by the empirical humanist system. This will enable governments to ban destructive or suicidal wars, foster planetary care, limit the climate change, and so on.

The union of humanist democratic countries would bring a new spirit of kinship, fostering only the best human emotions and behavior toward fellow humans. Taking human nature into account, humanism is the worldview most likely to win social approval. Humanists must now begin their work. The enemies of humanism are working to destroy everything of good value. We must move toward a world without dictatorships and war. This will bring self-actualization to everyone as the greater good.

It all started in modern times with Kurt Goldstein and Abraham Maslow, who wrote about a new definition of humanism. Humanism is just a new secular ideology derived from human nature—that is, the drive toward self-actualization and the great religions. However, neither Goldstein nor Maslow has shown us the detailed organization of how the drive toward self-actualization actually works—and how the various parts of the EP work collectively to produce self-actualization. That task remains mine, as I presented it in the first book of this trilogy. It is also summarized in the united theory of motivation contained in appendix A of this book. It is called the entelechial process (EP). This is followed by the humanist code (see appendix B), also contained in the first book. The humanist code is derived from the unified theory of motivation, or human nature. It is designed to objectively and scientifically distinguish good from evil and to tell us how far we can go with such ideas as religion, sovereignty, capitalism, socialism, feminism, the mining of natural resources, and so on but also when we should abandon them. What works for the EP at one time, after all, might no longer work at some other time or place.

After designing the technology of self-actualization, we must design social institutions that lead to the self-actualization of the greatest number of people. This is something entirely new to our social structures. We must not be so enamored with any social system or idea to the extent of harming the organism of self-actualization. Eventually, we must design international institutions to promote self-actualization at the global level. This means a humanistic and democratic world federalism: the beginning of the end for all authoritarian structures, wars, grinding poverty, genocides, endless refugees, and all international evils that a humanist code condemns. This would mean abandoning our existing attachments to sovereignty in favor of the greater good of a humanist and, therefore, democratic world federalism.

The pursuit of world federalism follows the classical motivation of the carrot and the stick. The carrot is represented by greater democratic powers, greater prosperity, and opportunities for development. It guarantees the entire set of humanist rights too: the assurance of peace and the supremacy of democracy. Moreover, it brings under greater control climate change and other problems concerning the health of the planet. It gives democracy the greatest opportunity to flourish instead of authoritarianism. The stick, in this case, is the common threat of tyranny and terrorism and the heavy cost of flash-fire wars and species-destroying conflicts.

Both the carrot and the stick are present, which bodes well for the rise of humanist and democratic world federalism. We need nothing more than this.

In the age of humanism, self-actualization is the central goal. We can modify or abandon such sovereignty, nationalism, and even religion in favor of self-actualization. We have a better and more enduring guide.

Afterwards

Anatomy of the Good Life

The good life is built around self-actualization within the context of the humanist code. The primary task in the first twenty years of life is the choice of the right career or vocation (constant B2). It would be the foundation of the good life. A person who does his work well receives a special recognition from society, no matter how great or modest the work is. Vocational excellence is most important for social creditability and respect.

This is a very important step in building the good life. If one chooses the wrong occupation, he or she will not be able to maintain a social structure that commands respect including self-confidence. Therefore, one should not be tempted to chose a career or vocation haphazardly or without due care. Everything falls to the ground around him without a solid vocation to turn to in case of a hard knock.

Following the choice of the right vocation it assumes the right education and all other knowledge listed in it as essential to self-actualization, with the choice of the vocation is still dominant and a number one issue for all youths before the age of twenty.

The second stage of development towards the good life is the social factor and support. The individual can only obtain recognition and support if he is professionally competent. It is from this position that he can obtain the support and joint action from society. This is the time between twenty and fifty years where the individual must devote himself to a social cause compatible with the humanist ideals and dear to his heart. The aim is to promote the humanist society and to help others so that they in turn could help him grow stronger.

The third stage is over fifty where the individuals' service to the community is at its strongest and most potent state. The aim is always the promotion of humanism extending beyond the range of local communities, even through the international arena. The unified theory of motivation contains all other aspects that would lead to the good life.

APPENDIX A

The Unified Theory of Motivation

The unified theory of motivation contains the entire universe of motivations and instincts that represent human nature and, thus, the drive for self-actualization.

This universe of motivation has four major constants or divisions:

1. Major constant A represents all *knowledge* that is necessary and available for self-actualization.
2. Major constant B represents all *behaviors* that are required for self-actualization and possible methods by which to achieve them.
3. Major constant C represents the desire to survive and maintain the body safety, health, and comfort.
4. Major constant D, on the other hand, represents the essential reaction (D1) and pathogenesis (D2).

These four major constants represent all motivations. They cannot be more than what they are. They cannot be less or other than what they are. They can be subdivided, however, into many smaller constants, which I call minor constants. For the purpose of this work, these smaller constants are as follows:

Minor constants A1 (collective conscience) and A2 (individual conscience), the axioma complex, represent all religious and political ideas that govern the lives and commerce of any community or nation. It includes religious, legal, and ethical rules. It governs the psyche. It links people together and sets them apart in the case of different religions or political ideology. It is the most decisive and most powerful motivational system. There has been no social events throughout history without an axioma complex of some kind. Primitive societies have their own value system as well and, in fact, no social system has been found without one. People sometimes risk their lives to defend its propagation. This, in fact, is how nations are formed.

Constant A2, the personal value system or conscience, represents personal values as distinct from communal ones. People can have values that differ from those of their communities and show up in particular behaviors that are different from collective ones.

Constant A1 and A2 are special in one way. They deal with axioms only, not facts. They accept whatever suits their purposes. Facts do not count here, only the *implications*. Thus, we have no proof of the existence of God, but people follow him anyway because God is an axiom and, therefore, requires no verification. In this case, only implications count. The worship of God is a primary source of self-actualization. It is needed to confirm our values and our links to the universe. Indeed, facts are totally alien to the axioma complex. This is worth remembering.

As we said, the axioma complex, consisting of minor constant A1 and minor constant A2, is in the form of axioms and plays that role, as distinct from facts. All ideas, commandments, historical events, ethical propositions, and all ideas at that level form the axioms of a logical-deductive system. Hence, these axioms are not verified. They only use this to draw implications leading to a given goal in behavioral reality. To that extent, they are considered to be true—that is, true to achieving their goal. In the case of humanism, the truth must lead to the self-actualization for the greatest number of people within the context of the humanist code (see appendix B).

Constant A3, self-knowledge or identity, represents personal knowledge. This knowledge centers on the vocations or jobs of men and the family lives of women. In addition, it contains other aspects of the personality.

Constant A4, vocational knowledge and skill, contains all the vocational and avocational skills required to make a living (e.g., medical or architectural knowledge required by professionals).

Constant A5 includes knowledge of self-actualization as the primary lifeforce of everyone and therefore of human nature, how to achieve it, and the essential human rights that follow from it. This would be a major constant for humanist democracy as a function of self-actualization.

Constant A6 involves concern for and knowledge of the planet with respect to the universe. This requires all available knowledge of both the planet and the universe. It requires people to care for the planet and all life.

Constant B1 involves the need for education. Self-actualization implies the use of skills for the benefit of humankind. This requires enough education to acquire specialized skills. Education should be compatible with the personal aptitude and ambitions. It is a basic right (to the extent that community resources are adequate).

Constant B2 involves the quest for a vocation. This is the primary channel of self-actualization for man and a second one, though essential, for women. Generally speaking, women fall behind men in vocational achievements not because women are less capable than men but because they are less motivated by nature than men. Female bodies motivate women to have children and care for them. But women should have the right to enter any profession as a vital function of their quest for self-actualization.

Constant B3 involves reproduction. This is the primary

channel of self-actualization for women and the secondary one, though essential, for men. The complementarity between men and women makes interdependence possible and family life workable.

Constant B4 is the constant of social relations. No one can live entirely alone. All people need social contact, such as friends, allies, partners, and coworkers. Maintaining friendships in particular is a necessary part of self-actualization.

Constant B5 involves participation in a preferably humanistic and democratic government. This is among the most important motivations. Only a government that is dedicated to the self-actualization for the greatest number of people can claim legitimacy. By nature, most people oppose any government that does not fulfill this purpose. Those who are lucky enough to enjoy democratic governments consider themselves happy and free. Therefore, democracy is a function of the technology of self-actualization. Those who are not consider themselves deprived. This is why dictatorships do not last, as they go against human nature.

Constant C1 is the universal need for food, which remains a strong constant of all life. No other constant can be satisfied without enough food in the belly.

Constant C2 is the desire for sex. Although sex makes reproduction possible, it satisfies other needs as well.

Constant C3 is the need for self-defense against enemies either human or nonhuman.

Constant C4 includes the need to maintain physical health and comfort: good housing, furniture, clothes, heating in winter, cooling in summer, sleep, and anything else that is not included in the previous three constants, relative to physical well-being.

Constant D1 includes essential reactions, such as fear, pride, pain, melancholy, and shame. Its function is to deter behavior that leads to injury, self-destruction, or antisocial action and that is, therefore, contrary to self-actualization. All events that knowingly do not benefit or answer the needs of self-actualization will register relative to this constant and in order to deter them. This is the negative side of the conscience.

Constant D2 is the constant of pathology. It contains all behaviors and thoughts that are contrary to self-actualization and, therefore, to whatever is negative or self-destructive. This constant acquires its power, in part, from the frustration or blockages of any of the preceding sixteen minor constants. It might be biologically caused too.

Indeed, this constant acquires its power from the failure in any part of the entelechial process (EP). The latter is like an organization with various departments. All should be working together to produce the desired results. The EP is a natural given and universal. Therefore, it must not be denied or improperly treated. It is an art as well as a science. Like medicine, for its data, it depends on experience, trial, and error. It is the heart of human nature. Therefore, the good life depends on the best possible management of the EP.

On the other hand, Sigmund Freud has postulated as a distinct instinct a death wish both individually and collectively, one that appears under special and extreme circumstances. The latter occurs among powerful dictators who fail to achieve their convoluted goals through brutal force and lies. This would make it more important than ever that the safety of the species be assured through purely humanistic social organizations.

APPENDIX B

The Humanist Code

I have developed a humanist code containing the ethical and legal principles that would be necessary for any humanist society. The humanist code tells us, on a scientific basis, precisely the definition of good and evil and the degree of their effectiveness. It likewise tells us how far we can take a good idea or behavior before modifying or abandoning it. This is completely new and can only be derived from the entelechial process (see appendix A). We can arrive at these principles directly from human nature. And we can do so now that we know how the entelechial process actually works. My goal, then, is to transform both ethics and law into hard and reliable sciences that are derived from human nature.

The various world religions have already established many of these principles. The Universal Declaration of Human Rights, published by the United Nations in 1948, has added others. But we must accept even those rights on faith, as it were, because they do not rely on scientific evidence about human nature. Like any religious texts, but without even a coherent philosophical context, the declaration simply declares that this or that is a right, a duty, a truth. Whether religious or secular, documents of this kind are likely to be misunderstood or misused, and they have indeed been so historically.

What we need is an external standard by which to evaluate these principles and values. I refer once again to science, but I refer more specifically to the social sciences. Psychologists can tell us a great deal about the way people think and behave. So can sociologists and anthropologists. With their studies in mind, we can make sensible choices. Ways of thinking and behaving that are likely to prove beneficial to most people are morally good from this perspective and should, therefore, be encouraged legally. Ways of thinking or behaving that are unlikely to prove beneficial are immoral and should be illegal as well. As a humanist, I would define both ethics and law as social sciences and make it possible for us to build a humanist society through hard science.

In that case, we should test religious insights in the hope that many will prove useful and first establish continuity with familiar traditions. We would have to discard those that do not prove useful. The validity of any principle lies not in its intrinsic truth or authority, much less on the intrinsic truth or authority of any religion, but on its likely contribution to building a humanist society and to opposing antihumanist regimes or movements. The humanist code is not a collection of doctrines, in other words, but a logical-deductive system that is based on knowledge of human nature—although it confirms many religious insights that our ancestors observed or intuited over many centuries of human experience. All of the world's religions have some humanist values.

One important task, therefore, is to translate those religions into secular terms and thus make them available to humanists and to society as a whole. Here, then, are the religious axioms that require translation into humanism.

Axiom 1: God created the universe and continues to guide it in beneficial ways.

Axiom 2: We are among God's most important creations; each of us bears the divine image, and each is endowed with a unique entelechy. Human self-actualization is, therefore, also divine self-actualization.

Axiom 3:   God has granted everyone the right to self-actualization, which should be limited only in the interest of someone else's right. In other words, society is more important than any of its parts. This is the first principle of justice or social humanism.

Axiom 4:   As part of the divine plan, God requires us to do two things. First, we must establish social institutions, including governments, that lead to the self-actualization for as many people as possible. Second, we must oppose tyranny as a violation of self-actualization. In other words, God regards authoritarianism as the worst of all sins.

Axiom 5:   Something innate and known only to God survives after death. God will keep faith until the end of time with those who serve him in truth.

Theorems

1. Everyone has an equal right to self-actualization within the context of the humanist code.
2. The function of government is the self-actualization for the greatest number of people within the context of the humanist code.
3. Humanist democracy is the basic right of everyone and of every nation.
4. Authoritarian systems violate human nature and have no right to exist. They foster criminal acts.
5. The use of any religious or political ideology to justify an authoritarian system should be outlawed.
6. The only correct interpretation of any religious injunction is one that fosters the humanist code and therefore nature itself.

7. Self-actualization involves all aspects of life, which are listed in the unified theory of motivation (see appendix A).

8. No loss should prohibit the normal expression of any behavioral constant, each of which is listed in the unified theory of motivation.

9. People are custodians of the natural environment and are, therefore, responsible for its integrity and usefulness in future generations. They are, therefore, obliged to form institutions that can accomplish these goals and the different circumstances.

10. Wanton destruction of the natural environment should be outlawed.

11. Every social or structural organization that leads to a higher degree of self-actualization has priority over any that delivers less self-actualization.

APPENDIX C

Self-Actualization and the Matrix of all Human Sciences

Self-actualization is a natural given and the matrix of all the human sciences. It touches on everything we do and do not do. Every action taken by anyone or not taken must affect self-actualization in one way or another. Therefore, world organization, not derived from the entelechial process is at best faulty or irrelevant. This is the political situation now which is confusing and dangerous. Political organizations which are not based on self-actualization as the central issue of human existence, leads not only to confusion but to conflict some of which in extreme cases leads to war. At this time the world simply cannot afford wars based on weapons of mass destruction.

By taking self-actualization as the central issue, first for the individual and then for society and then for the whole world, solutions even to the most difficult and complicated problems become soluble due to a single value system based on human nature and accepted by all. This is what the humanist code does. Values of good and evil flow naturally if self-actualization is the central matrix of all human activity. A world order based on self-actualization as the central matrix leads at once to a logical solution. When not so ordered it leads to irreconcilable differences and conflicts. It simply does not work. This work has shown how to achieve self-actualization for the individual, for society as a whole and for the whole world starting from this point in history going forward towards the future. It requires no super human efforts. In fact self-actualization as I have shown comes naturally and pleasantly to everyone. It requires a humanist democracy and rejects all authoritarian rules which violate self-actualization. This is the only way the world can be ordered and nations can live in peace and cooperation with each other.

Because, for the same reason no other solution would work and would eventually lead to conflicts and war.

The first task of any individual anywhere in the world must be to achieve self-actualization by discovering and realizing its full potential of his or her self-actualization. This gives him or her the necessary power to fight for what is good and avoid what is evil throughout life. This comes automatically to all self-actualizers. The second is organizing society in such a manner as to lead to self-actualization for the greatest number of people. This has been given in the second book of this trilogy – The Humanist Society. The third course was described in this book on how to achieve the self-actualization for the greatest number of people throughout the world by organizing the institutions to the goal of human harmony and peace.

Glossary

axioma complex: The religio-political principles that govern a nation's laws, ethics, and general rules of behavior. Essentially it consists of religion and (or) secular ideology, such as the various religions in the United States and, more important, in its secular Constitution and Bill of Rights. They define the character of the nation and explain its behavior.

axiopathy: The use of the axioma complex to commit high crimes in the name of religion or secular ideology. This is sometimes done through perverted interpretation of the scriptures or secular ideology through an established political power to maintain an authoritarian system.

constant: A combination of instinct for or a common purpose, such as the desire to maintain good health, have a roof over one's head, and live comfortably.

entelechy: A Greek term meaning behavior that comes from within.

entelechial process: Derived from the Greek word *entelechy*, issuing from the inside of the organism. For example, the desire for certain knowledge, food, or sex is universal and does not depend on human volition but is biologically based. It is the specialized nature of every living thing.

humanism: All behaviors leading to self-actualization in line with the humanist code.

humanist code: A code of behavior leading to the self-actualization for the greatest number of people as derived from the great religions and secular ideology insofar as the achievement of self-actualization is concerned. It tells us how to achieve self-actualization for the greatest number of people in any community or nation. It is likewise intended to define good and evil on a scientific basis and to tell us how far we can follow a good idea or behavior before modifying or abandoning it. The humanist code contains all rights that are derived from human nature and are, therefore, universal.

humanist spirituality: It is the healthy spirituality as distinguished from the sick axiopathy (see above). It is the spirituality of Abraham Maslow as found among self-actualizers. It is distinguished by a strong sense of purpose, inner strength, and great achievement. It is not related to organized religion but is a natural given to all humans.

law of devolution: Humanist behavior leads to individual self-actualization and social strength. Contrary behavior leads to pathology, self-destruction, despotism, or other crimes and failures. The law of devolution states that unless individual and social behavior is guided toward humanist goals, behavior can become pathogenic or authoritarian.

two-dimensional behavior of ends and means: It became necessary for the establishment of verifiable technology of self-actualization to distinguish clearly between ends and means in some behavior. Ends and means are presented as a ratio similar to the current ratios in cost accounting, which is sales / cost of sales, which measures the efficiency of the operation. In this work, the ratio has no quantifiable significance but defines the relationship only between clear ends and means respectively.

unified theory of motivation: The unified theory of motivation is in line with the theories of Kurt Goldstein and Abraham Maslow, who postulated that self-actualization is the one and only instinct that governs human behavior. However, neither Goldstein nor Maslow told us *how* to achieve self-actualization. This work extends their idea forward as to how to achieve self-actualization. (An abbreviated form of this theory is contained in appendix A; the full theory and technology is contained in book 1 of this trilogy.)

Index

www.ingramcontent.com/pod-product-compliance
Lightning Source LLC
Chambersburg PA
CBHW030517290526
45786CB00004B/1506